INSTANT POT SLOW COOKER COOKBOOK

The Top Set It and Forget It Recipes for Everyday Cooking

James Diamond

Copyright © 2017 by James Diamond - All rights reserved.

No part of this publication may be reproduced, stored in a retrieval system, or transmitted, in any form or by any means, electronic, mechanical, photocopying, recording or otherwise, without the prior written permission of the author and the publishers.

This document is geared towards providing exact and reliable information in regards to the topic and issue covered. The publication is sold with the idea that the publisher is not required to render accounting, officially permitted, or otherwise, qualified services. If advice is necessary, legal or professional, a practiced individual in the profession should be ordered.

The information provided herein is stated to be truthful and consistent, in that any liability, in terms of inattention or otherwise, by any usage or abuse of any policies, processes, or directions contained within is the solitary and utter responsibility of the recipient reader. Under no circumstances will any legal responsibility or blame be held against the publisher for any reparation, damages or monetary loss due to the information herein, either directly or indirectly.

The information herein is offered for informational purposes solely, and is universal as so. The presentation of the information is without contract or any type of guarantee assurance. The trademarks that are used are without any consent, and the publication of the trademark is without permission or backing by the trademark owner. All trademarks and brands within this book are for clarifying purposes only and are owned by the owners themselves, not affiliated with this document.

Disclaimer: This book is not affiliated with the official owner/trademark of Instant Pot. Instant Pot is the registered trademark of Double Insight Inc. Instant Pot was designed in Canada, with healthy living, green living and ethnic diversity in mind. All other trademarks are the property of their respective owners. James Diamond is not associated with any other product or vendor mentioned in this book.

Table of Contents

INTRODUCTION 7

CHAPTER 1 – BREAKFAST 9
    Apple Pie Oatmeal 9
    Bacon, Egg Casserole 10
    Blueberry Oatmeal 11
    Breakfast Quinoa 12
    French Toast Casserole 13
    Greek Egg Casserole 14
    Maple Hazelnut Oatmeal 15
    Pumpkin Bread 16
    Quinoa Energy Bar 18
    Sausage & Pepper Hash 20
    Sticky Pecan Buns 21
    Veggie Omelet 23

CHAPTER 2 – SOUPS, STEWS AND CHOWDERS 25
    Apple Parsnip Soup 25
    Autumn Minestrone 26
    Beef Osso Bucco 28
    Black Bean Chili 30
    Black Bean Soup 31
    Butternut Squash Stew 32
    Cheddar Chicken Chowder 33
    Chicken Chowder 34
    Chicken Dumpling Soup 35
    Potato Soup 36
    Provencal Beef Stew 37
    Rosemary Chicken Noodle Soup 39

CHAPTER 3 – POULTRY 40
    Chinese Sweet and Sour Chicken 40
    Creamy Lemon Chicken 41

Duck a l'Orange 43
Duck Cassoulet 44
Italian Turkey 45
Neapolitan Chicken Cacciatore 46
Paprika Chicken 48
Salsa Chicken 49
Spicy Chicken 50
Thanksgiving Turkey 51
Turkey Legs 52
Turkey Sausage Cassoulet 53

CHAPTER 4 – BEEF, PORK & LAMB 55
Barbecue Pulled Pork 55
Bolognese 56
Braised Beef Ragu 57
Coffee Braised Pot Roast 58
Lamb Ribs 59
Leg Of Lamb 60
Moroccan Lamb Tagine 61
Pork Roast 63
Red Curry Bison Short Ribs 64
Red Curry Pulled Pork 66
Rosemary Lamb 68
Sweet Tangy Short Ribs 69

CHAPTER 5 – VEGETARIAN & VEGAN 71
Barley Chickpea Risotto 71
Eggplant Parmesan 73
Picadillo Stuffed Peppers 74
Pinto Bean Sloppy Joe 76
Quinoa Black Bean Peppers 78
Root Vegetable Tagine 79
Sweet Potato 80
Vegan Jambalaya 81

Vegetable Curry 82
Vegetable Pot Pie 83
Vegetarian Curry 85
Vegetarian Lasagna 86

CHAPTER 6 – PASTA & GRAINS 88
Baked Spaghetti 88
Cheesy Noodle Casserole 89
Eggplant Ziti 90
Hungarian Beef Goulash 92
Macaroni and Cheese 94
Provincial Chicken 95
Quinoa and Sausage 96
Quinoa Casserole 97
Spaghetti 98
Spicy Lasagna 99
Wild Mushroom Alfredo 100
Wild Rice with Corn 101

CHAPTER 7 – SEAFOOD 102
Amazing Mussels 102
Fisherman's Wharf Seafood 104
Lemon and Herb Cod 105
Paella 106
Salmon 107
Seafood Stew 109
Shrimp and Grits 110
Shrimp Boil 111
Shrimp Creole 112
Shrimp Scampi 113
Spicy Citrus Fish 114
Steamed Mussels 115

CHAPTER 8 – DESSERTS 116
Caramel Pear Pudding Cake 116

Crustless Lemony Cheesecake 117
Ginger Orange Cheesecake 118
Hazelnut Pudding Cake 120
Orange Caramel Pudding Cake 121
Peach Graham Cracker Upside Down Cake 123
Peppermint Pretzel Candies 124
Pumpkin Pomegranate Cheesecake 125
Raspberry Fudge Brownies 126
Triple Chocolate Pudding Cake 127

INTRODUCTION

It shouldn't have to be said that the Instant Pot and slow cookers are a life savers. The main reason is that they give you delicious meals with little to no work required. They are also an easy way to have nutritious and delicious meals. You can use them all year round. And they're more energy efficient because they don't use as much energy as a conventional oven. It's a one pot clean up meal, and they can be transported easily. When was the last time you saw somebody carrying around an oven?

As I'm sure you know, the Instant Pot has several settings, one of which is a slow cooker setting, and that's the setting you will be using for all of recipes in this book. To help you out, I'm going to quickly go over how to use the slow cooker setting so that we're all on the same page.

With the slow cooker setting you get to cook for 2 to 10 hours, and set the heat on low, medium, or high.

To use the slow cooker setting, lock the lid in place and set the steam release to either one of the venting positions. Then select slow cook and set the amount of time you will need with the plus or minus button.

After that, press the adjust key to select the temperature. Each time you press adjust, the light will toggle from less, normal to more. That is the equivalent of low, medium, and high. Once you've done that, you're all done - sit back and let your Instant Pot work for you.

The following chapters will give your several recipes for you to use in your Instant Pot on the slow cook setting. There are plenty of books on this subject on the market, thanks again for choosing this one! I hope you enjoy making these recipes at home for you and your family. Every effort was made to ensure it is full of as much useful information as possible, please enjoy! And if you really liked this book, feel free to leave a comment.

CHAPTER 1 – BREAKFAST

Apple Pie Oatmeal

Total Preparation & Cook Time: 8 hours 15 Minutes

Servings – 5

Nutritional info: Calories: 180, Fats: 5g, Carbs: 31g, Protein: 5g, Sugar: 11g, Sodium: 135mg

Ingredients:

- splash lemon juice
- 1 tsp cinnamon
- 2 tbsp maple syrup
- ¼ tsp nutmeg
- 1 tsp coconut oil
- 2 apples, chopped
- 4 c almond milk
- 1 c steel-cut oats

Directions:

1. Place all of the ingredients in your pot. Stir everything together. Set to slow cook on low, and set to 8 hours, or set for 4 hours on high.
2. Stir everything again. Top with apples and peanut butter if desired.
3. Can be stored for a week in the fridge.

Bacon, Egg Casserole

Total Preparation & Cook Time: 5 hours

Servings – 8

Nutritional info: Calories: 342, Fats: 22g, Carbs: 14g, Protein: 21g, Sugar: 2g, Sodium: 648mg

Ingredients:

- cooking spray
- ¼ tsp pepper
- ½ tsp salt
- ½ c milk
- 12 eggs
- 6 green onions, sliced
- 8 oz cheddar cheese
- 8 slices bacon, cooked and chopped
- 20 oz bag hash browns

Directions:

1. Grease the pot with nonstick spray. Put half of you hash brown on the bottom. Then layer with half of the bacon and cheese, and the 1/3 of the onion. Repeat with remaining hash brown, then bacon, then cheese, and another third of the onion.

2. Whisk the pepper, salt, milk, and eggs together in a bowl. Pour over the hash brown layers. Set to slow cook. Set to low four to five hours, or two to three hours on high. Serve with extra onions.

Chapter 1 – Breakfast

Blueberry Oatmeal

Total Preparation & Cook Time: 2 hours 35 minutes

Servings – 4

Nutritional info: Calories: 240, Fats: 5g, Carbs: 45g, Protein: 6g, Sugar: 14g, Sodium: 133mg

Ingredients:

- 1 tsp vanilla
- 2 c blueberries
- 1 tbsp maple syrup
- 2 c water
- 2 c vanilla almond milk
- salt
- ½ tsp cinnamon
- ¼ c granola
- 2 tbsp ground flaxseed
- 1 c steel cut oats

Directions:

1. Spray pot with cooking spray.
2. Mix everything in the pot, minus the vanilla.
3. Set to slow cook. Set time to 7 hours on low, or 2 ½ hours on high. Mix in the vanilla and enjoy.

Breakfast Quinoa

Total Preparation & Cook Time: 3 hours 5 minutes

Servings – 5

Nutritional info: Calories: 293, Fats: 8g, Carbs: 48g, Protein: 9g, Sugar: 20g, Sodium: 224mg

Ingredients:

- ¼ tsp salt
- 1 tsp vanilla
- ¼ tsp nutmeg
- 2 tsp cinnamon
- apple, diced and peeled
- ¼ c
- 4 dates, chopped
- 3 c milk
- 1 c quinoa

Directions:

1. Place everything in your cooker.
2. Set slow cook. Set to low for 8 hours, or 2 hours on high. Make sure all liquid has absorbed.
3. If you want to cook it on low, set it before you go to bed, and you will have breakfast waiting when you get up.

French Toast Casserole

Total Preparation & Cook Time: 2 hours 40 minutes

Servings – 9

Nutritional info: Calories: 227, Fats: 7g, Carbs: 34g, Protein: 9g, Sugar: 19g, Sodium: 187mg

Ingredients:

- ½ tsp cinnamon
- 1/3 c diced pecans
- 2 tbsp honey
- 1 tsp lemon juice
- 3 tbsp honey
- 3 c diced apple pieces
- 1 ½ c milk
- 9 slices bread
- ½ tsp cinnamon
- 2 eggs
- 1 tsp vanilla
- 2 egg whites

Directions:

1. Mix the last 6 ingredients together in a bowl. Spray your cooker with cooking spray.

2. Toss the first 5 ingredients together and set aside.

3. Cut the bread in half (triangles). Place a layer of your triangles in the bottom of the pot. Top with ¼ of your apple mixture. Continue doing this until you have used all of your bread and top with the rest of the apple mixture.

4. Pour the eggs over the bread. Cover, set to slow cook, and set to high for two and a half hours, or low four hours. The bread should have time to absorb all of the liquid.

5. Serve with a drizzle of maple syrup.

Greek Egg Casserole

Total Preparation & Cook Time: 4 hours 5 minutes

Servings – 4-6

Nutritional info: Calories: 244, Fats: 16g, Carbs: 7g, Protein: 20g, Sugar: 4g, Sodium: 579mg

Ingredients:

- ½ c feta cheese
- 1 c sliced mushrooms
- 1 tsp garlic powder
- ½ c sun dried tomatoes
- 2 c spinach
- 1 tbsp onion powder
- ½ tsp salt
- 1 tsp pepper
- ½ c milk
- 12 eggs, whisked

Directions:

1. Mix together the pepper, salt, milk, and eggs.
2. Whisk in the garlic and onion powder.
3. Stir in the spinach, mushrooms, and tomatoes.
4. Pour this into you cooker. Sprinkle over the feta.
5. Set to slow cook for 4-6 hours on low.

Maple Hazelnut Oatmeal

Total Preparation & Cook Time: 7 hours 5 minutes

Servings – 4

Nutritional info: Calories: 358, Fats: 9g, Carbs: 62g, Protein: 8.9g, Sugar: 20g, Sodium: 226mg

Ingredients:

- 2 tbsp hazelnuts, chopped
- ½ tbsp butter, softened
- ¼ tsp cinnamon
- ¼ c maple syrup
- 1 ½ c fat free milk
- ¼ tsp salt
- 1 c steel cut oats
- 2 apples, peeled and diced
- cooking spray
- 2 tbsp brown sugar
- 1
- 1 ½ c water

Directions:

1. Boil the milk and the water together. Stir frequently.

2. Spray the cooker with nonstick spray. Pour the milk, apples, oats, sugar, butter, cinnamon, and salt in the cooker. Mix well. Set to slow cook for 7 hours on low. Oats should be tender when done.

3. Serve oatmeal with a sprinkle of hazelnuts and a drizzle of syrup.

Pumpkin Bread

Total Preparation & Cook Time: 3 hours 5 minutes

Servings – 16

Nutritional info: Calories: 159, Fats: 6.5g, Carbs: 21g, Protein: 4g, Sugar: 8g, Sodium: 70mg

Ingredients:

- 2 oz toasted pecan pieces
- 1 tbsp vanilla
- ¼ tsp sea salt
- ¼ c safflower oil
- 4 egg whites
- ½ c plain Greek yogurt
- ¼ tsp allspice
- ½ tsp ground cloves
- 1 c canned pumpkin
- ¼ tsp baking soda
- 2 tsp baking powder
- ¼ tsp nutmeg
- 1 ¾ c white whole wheat flour
- 1 tsp cinnamon
- ½ c dried cranberries
- ¾ c apple juice
- ½ tsp ground ginger
- ½ c maple sugar flakes
- cooking spray

Directions:

1. Coat a loaf pan with nonstick spray.
2. Mix the cranberries and apple juice in a pot. Allow to boil. Remove from heat and cool 10 minutes.
3. Whisk all of the dry ingredients and spices together.

4. In another bowl mix together the vanilla, oil, egg whites, yogurt, pumpkin, and cranberry mixture. Pour wet mixture into dry mixture and combine. Fold in the pecans. Pour into the prepared pan and gently tap on the counter to level.

5. Place a rack or trivet in your pot and set the pan on top. Set to slow cook for 2 ¾ hours on high. A toothpick should come out clean.

Quinoa Energy Bar

Total Preparation & Cook Time: 4 hours 10 minutes

Servings – 8

Nutritional info: Calories: 174, Fats: 8.4g, Carbs: 20.1g Protein: 6.1g, Sugar: 9.1g, Sodium: 39mg

Ingredients:

- 2 tbsp chia seeds
- 2 eggs
- 1/3 c dried apples, chopped
- ½ c raisins
- salt
- 1 c vanilla almond milk
- 2 tbsp almond butter
- 1/3 c quinoa
- ½ tsp cinnamon
- 1/3 c toasted almonds, chopped
- 2 tbsp maple syrup

Directions:

1. Spray your cooker with nonstick spray and place parchment paper in the bottom. Spray again with nonstick spray.
2. In a heat safe bowl, combine the syrup and almond butter. Microwave in 20 second increments to make creamy.
3. Stir in cinnamon, salt, and milk. Mix until it is complete incorporated.
4. Mix in eggs, and stir in all the rest of the ingredients.

5. Pour into the cooker. Set to slow cook for 4 hours on low heat.

6. Slide a knife along the edges and ease out bars. Set in the fridge to cool.

7. When the bars have cooled, cut into individual bars.

Sausage & Pepper Hash

Total Preparation & Cook Time: 5 hours 20 minutes

Servings – 10

Nutritional info: Calories: 131, Fats: 3g, Carbs: 18g, Protein: 6g, Sugar: 7g, Sodium: 220mg

Ingredients:

- 2 tsp fresh tarragon
- ½ c Swiss cheese
- 1 ½ c chopped red sweet peppers
- ¼ c chicken broth
- ½ tsp pepper
- ½ tsp thyme
- 1 ½ lbs red potatoes
- cooking spray
- 1 ½ c onion, sliced
- 1 tsp olive oil
- 12 oz package smoked sausage, sliced

Directions:

1. Coat your cooker with nonstick spray. Mix together pepper, thyme, potatoes, onion, and sausage. Pour in the broth.

2. Set to slow cook. Set time to five to six hours on low, or 2 ½ -3 hours on high. Mix in the peppers and cheese.

3. Serve with sprinkle of tarragon.

Sticky Pecan Buns

Total Preparation & Cook Time: 2 hours 40 minutes

Servings – 12

Nutritional info: Calories: 154, Fats: 4.9g, Carbs: 26.2g Protein: 2.9g, Sugar: 11.6g, Sodium: 54.9mg

Ingredients:

Filling:

- ½ tbsp butter, melted
- 1 ½ tsp cinnamon
- 3 tbsp maple syrup

Sauce:

- 2 tbsp milk
- ¼ c chopped pecans
- 4 tbsp maple syrup
- 2 tbsp butter

Dough:

- ¼ tsp salt
- ½ tbsp butter
- 1 tsp vanilla
- 1 ½ -2 c whole wheat flour
- 4 tbsp maple syrup
- 2 ¼ tsp yeast
- 6 tbsp milk

Directions:

1. Coat your cooker with cooking spray.

2. For the dough: Mix the vanilla, butter, syrup, and milk in a glass bowl. Microwave in 20 second intervals to melt the butter; stirring after each interval. Mix in the yeast and let proof for 10- 15 minutes. It should become frothy.

3. Stir in ½ cup flour at a time just until the dough stops sticking to your bowl. Knead your dough on a floured surface until dough springs back at your touch. Let rest what the filling and sauce is prepared.

4. For the caramel sauce: mix syrup, milk, and butter in a saucepan. Cook on medium-low until it thickens and darkens in color. Pour over the bottom of cooker. Top with pecans.

5. For the filling: mix together the cinnamon and syrup.

6. On a floured surface, roll or pat out the dough. Roll out into a 10 by 14 inch rectangle. Brush over with melted butter. Brush with the cinnamon-syrup mixture. Roll the dough up on the long edge. Slice dough into 12 rolls. Place in the cooker.

7. Cover and set to keep warm. Let sit 45 minutes. The rolls should double in size. Then set to slow cook. Set to 1 ½ on low. Uncover and let cook 10 minutes. Carefully take the rolls out.

Chapter 1 – Breakfast

Veggie Omelet

Total Preparation & Cook Time: 2 hours 15 minutes

Servings – 4

Nutritional info: Calories: 139, Fats: 7g, Carbs: 10g, Protein: 10g, Sugar: 5g, Sodium: 226mg

Ingredients:

- parsley
- onion, chopped
- 1/8 tsp chili powder
- 1 onion, chopped
- 1 c broccoli florets
- tomato, chopped
- shredded cheese
- 1 clove garlic, minced
- 1 red bell pepper, sliced
- 1/8 tsp garlic powder
- pepper
- ¼ tsp salt
- ½ c milk
- 6 eggs

Directions:

1. Grease your cooker with nonstick spray.
2. Combine the pepper, chili powder, salt, garlic powder, milk, and eggs.
3. Stir in the garlic, onions, pepper, and broccoli.
4. Pour into the cooker. Set to slow cook. Set to two hours on high. Make sure the eggs are set before serving.

5. Top with cheese and cover for a few minutes to melt.
6. Cut into 8 sections.
7. Serve with parsley, chopped onions and tomatoes.

CHAPTER 2 – SOUPS, STEWS AND CHOWDERS

Apple Parsnip Soup

Total Preparation & Cook Time: 10 hours

Servings – 6

Nutritional info: Calories: 169, Fats: 1g, Carbs: 38g, Protein: 30g, Sugar: 14g, Sodium: 252mg

Ingredients:

- ½ tsp salt
- 3 cans chicken broth
- 1 onion, chopped
- 2 apples, peeled and quartered
- 6 parsnips, peeled and chunked

Directions:

1. Put all of the ingredients in your cooker.
2. Mix everything well.
3. Cover and set to slow cook. Set for 10-12 hours on low. Parsnips should be tender.
4. Let it cool for 10 minutes.
5. Pour everything in a blender, and blend until smooth.

Autumn Minestrone

Total Preparation & Cook Time: 9 hours 20 minutes

Servings – 6

Nutritional info: Calories: 279, Fats: 9g, Carbs: 39g, Protein: 20g, Sugar: 10g, Sodium: 682mg

Ingredients:

- 2 tbsp water
- ¼ tsp pepper
- ¼ tsp salt
- 3 tbsp EVOO
- ¼ c parmesan
- 1/3 c parsley
- 1 tbsp garlic, minced
- 1 leek, sliced
- 2 c coleslaw mix
- 1 c basil
- 1 parsnip, peeled and quartered
- 2 turnips, peeled and chunked
- 1 can diced tomatoes
- 3 c butternut squash
- 2 cans chicken broth
- 2 cans cannellini beans

Directions:

1. Combine half of the garlic, leek, coleslaw, parsnip, turnips, tomatoes and juice, squash, broth, and beans in your cooker.

2. Cover and set to slow cook. Set for 7-9 hours on low. Vegetables should be tender.

Chapter 2 – Soups, Stews And Chowders

3. In a blender, mix together the rest of the garlic, water, pepper, salt, oil, cheese, parsley, and basil. Blend until completely smooth.

4. Place in a container and refrigerate until the soup is done.

5. Serve soup with a drizzle of the basil mixture.

Beef Osso Bucco

Total Preparation & Cook Time: 8 hours 30 minutes

Servings – 8

Nutritional info: Calories: 207, Fats: 6g, Carbs: 10.8g, Protein: 24.3g, Sugar: 2g, Sodium: 557mg

Ingredients:

- 1 tbsp garlic, minced
- 6 tbsp chopped parsley
- 8 plum tomatoes
- ¾ c celery, chopped
- bay leaf
- ¾ tsp pepper
- 2 tsp cornstarch
- 1 tbsp lemon zest
- ½ c dry red wine
- ¼ oz dry porcini mushrooms, chopped
- 1 c beef stock
- 8 garlic cloves, crushed
- 2 tbsp tomato paste
- ¾ c carrot, chopped
- 2 c onion, sliced
- cooking spray
- 1 tbsp oil, divide
- 3 lbs bone in beef shanks
- 1 ¾ tsp salt, divided

Directions:

1. Season beef with ½ teaspoon of salt and brown in a skillet. Coat your cooker with nonstick spray. Place in the beef, garlic, tomato paste, carrot, celery, and onion. Mix together the mushrooms and stock and pour into

Chapter 2 – Soups, Stews And Chowders

pot. Then add the bay leaf, pepper, cornstarch, and wine.

2. Put the tomatoes on a cookie sheet. Place under a broiler for 8 minutes. Put the tomatoes on top of the beef and press to crush them and release juices.

3. Cover, set to slow cook, and set for 8 hours on low. Take out the beef and scrape the meat off of the bones. Take out the bay leaf and add the beef and remaining salt into the pot.

4. Stir everything together. Mix the garlic, parsley, and zest. Sprinkle mixture on top of soup.

Black Bean Chili

Total Preparation & Cook Time: 3 hours 10 minutes

Servings – 6

Nutritional info: Calories: 228, Fats: 7g, Carbs: 31.5g, Protein: 12g, Sugar: 0g, Sodium: 980mg

Ingredients:

- ¼ tsp pepper
- 1 tsp cocoa powder
- 2 garlic cloves, chopped
- ½ tsp salt
- 1 bunch scallions, chopped
- 1 tbsp chili powder
- 1 c corn
- 2 cans diced tomatoes with chilies
- 1 tsp cumin
- 2 cans black beans

Directions:

1. Combine everything in your cooker. Set to slow cook to high for 3-4 hours.
2. You can serve the chili with sour cream, tortilla chips and cilantro.

Black Bean Soup

Total Preparation & Cook Time: 18 hours 10 minutes

Servings – 6

Nutritional info: Calories: 286, Fats: 2.2g, Carbs: 51.1g Protein: 17g, Sugar: 0g, Sodium: 697mg

Ingredients:

- 3 tbsp sour cream
- 1 tbsp cumin
- ¼ c cilantro
- 2 tbsp lime juice
- 1 c water
- 1 serrano chili, chopped
- 2 c onion, chopped
- 3 bay leaves
- 4 c vegetable broth
- 1 tsp salt
- 1 lb dried black beans

Directions:

1. Sort through and rinse the beans. Put them in a bowl and cover complete with water. The beans have to sit for 8 hours. Drain out the water.
2. Mix together the chili, bay leaves, cumin, water, onion, broth, and beans in your cooker. Set to slow cook for 10 hours on low. Remove the bay leaves. Mix in salt and juice.

Butternut Squash Stew

Total Preparation & Cook Time: 8 hours 10 minutes

Servings – 8

Nutritional info: Calories: 220, Fats: 1g, Carbs: 48g, Protein: 9g, Sugar: 9g, Sodium: 895mg

Ingredients:

- pepper
- 1 onion, chopped
- salt
- bay leaf
- 4 garlic cloves, chopped
- ½ c pearl barley
- 2 tsp paprika
- 6 c vegetable broth
- 2 tsp cumin
- 1 green bell pepper, chopped
- 1 c dry kidney beans
- 1 tbsp chili powder
- 2 celery stalks, chopped
- 2 carrots, chopped
- 28 oz can fire roasted tomatoes
- 6 c butternut squash, chopped

Directions:

1. Let the beans soak in water overnight.
2. Throw everything into your cooker and mix together. Set to slow cook for 8 hours on low. Season with pepper and salt if needed.

Chapter 2 – Soups, Stews And Chowders

Cheddar Chicken Chowder

Total Preparation & Cook Time: 8 hours 30 minutes

Servings – 7

Nutritional info: Calories: 306, Fats: 7.5g, Carbs: 33.7g
Protein: 25g, Sugar: 0g, Sodium: 376mg

Ingredients:

- ¼ tsp pepper
- ½ tsp salt
- 4 ½ c chicken broth
- ¾ c cheddar cheese
- 2 c 2% milk
- 1 c red bell pepper, diced
- 1 c onion, chopped
- ½ c AP flour
- 2 ¼ c corn
- 1 lb boneless chicken breasts, diced
- 1 ¾ c red potatoes, peeled and diced
- 2 garlic cloves, minced
- cooking spray
- 2 bacon slices

Directions:

1. Place garlic, pepper, onion, chicken, milk, potatoes, broth, and corn in the cooker. Mix everything together. Set to slow cook for 8 hours on low.

2. While the chowder cooks. Cook the bacon in a skillet, crumble and set to the side.

3. Once done, mix in pepper, salt, and cheese. Serve with the bacon.

Chicken Chowder

Total Preparation & Cook Time: 3 hours 10 minutes

Servings – 8

Nutritional info: Calories: 240, Fats: 7.8g, Carbs: 19.4g, Protein: 23.7g, Sugar: 2.8g, Sodium: 859mg

Ingredients:

- ½ c half and half
- 1 small onion, chopped
- 2 celery stalks, chopped
- 1 tsp dill
- 1 ½ c chicken broth
- 1 ½ lbs chicken, diced
- 2 tbsp butter
- 2 c frozen corn
- 2 carrots, chopped
- 2 cans cream of potato soup

Directions:

1. Place everything in the cooker, except half and half, and stir to mix well. Set to slow cook for 3-4 hours on low. Chicken shouldn't be pink and veggies should be soft
2. Once done, mix in the half and half.

Chapter 2 – Soups, Stews And Chowders

Chicken Dumpling Soup

Total Preparation & Cook Time: 6 hours 15 minutes

Servings – 6

Nutritional info: Calories: 250, Fats: 3g, Carbs: 32g, Protein: 26.5g, Sugar: 0g, Sodium: 417.5mg

Ingredients:

- ½ c 1 % milk
- 1 lb boneless chicken breasts, diced
- 1 ½ c biscuit mix
- 1 onion, chopped
- 10 oz frozen vegetables
- 2 cans chicken broth

Directions:

1. Put the onion, veggies, broth, and chicken in the cooker and mix well.
2. Set to slow cook. Set time to 5 hours if on low or 2 ½ hours if on high.
3. Mix together the milk and biscuit mix. Drop spoonfuls into the soup. Cook for another hour on high. Season with some pepper.

Potato Soup

Total Preparation & Cook Time: 8 hours 40 minutes

Servings – 8

Nutritional info: Calories: 259, Fats: 6.4g, Carbs: 37.8g, Protein: 13.2g, Sugar: 0g, Sodium: 683mg

Ingredients:

- 4 tsp chives, chopped
- ½ c sour cream
- 4 oz cheddar cheese
- 2 c 1 % milk
- ½ tsp pepper
- ½ tsp salt
- 2 cans chicken broth
- ½ c water
- cooking spray
- 3 lbs potatoes, peeled and diced
- 1 c onion, chopped
- 3 bacon slices

Directions:

1. Crisp the bacon in a skillet. Place onions in the drippings and cook for a few minutes.
2. Put the potatoes and onion in the cooker that has been sprayed with nonstick spray. Mix the pepper, salt broth and water together and pour over potatoes. Set to slow cook for 8 hours on low.
3. Take a potato masher and mash the soup. Then mix in ¾ cup of cheese and the milk. Turn the temp to high and cook another 20 minutes. Serve with sour cream, cheese, chives, and bacon.

Chapter 2 – Soups, Stews And Chowders

Provencal Beef Stew

Total Preparation & Cook Time: 8 hours 31 minutes

Servings – 6

Nutritional info: Calories: 271, Fats: 8.9g, Carbs: 16.5g, Protein: 31.1g, Sugar: 0g, Sodium: 499mg

Ingredients:

- 2 c carrot, sliced
- 3 c zucchini, sliced
- 1 can diced tomatoes
- 3 thyme sprigs
- 1 tsp salt, divided
- 3 bay leaves
- 1 c beef brother
- ¼ c dry red wine
- 8 garlic cloves, crushed
- 2 tbsp tomato paste
- 2 onions, cut into wedges
- 2 tbsp AP flour
- ½ tsp pepper, divided
- 1 ½ lbs boneless chuck roast, cubed
- 2 tsp olive oil

Directions:

1. Heat a skillet with oil. Season beef cubes with some pepper and salt. Coat the beef in flour. Place beef in pan and brown. Put the browned beef in the cooker.

2. Place the garlic onion to the pan and let it cook. Deglaze the pan with the wine. Place the win mixture in your cooker along with the carrots, zucchini, tomatoes, thyme, bay leaves, tomato paste, and broth. Mix together.

3. Set to slow cook for 8 hours on low. Mix in the rest of the pepper and salt. Take out the bay leaves and thyme. Stir and serve.

Chapter 2 – Soups, Stews And Chowders

Rosemary Chicken Noodle Soup

Total Preparation & Cook Time: 8 hours 31 minutes

Servings – 10

Nutritional info: Calories: 266, Fats: 5.4g, Carbs: 21.2g, Protein: 33.6g, Sugar: 0g, Sodium: 556mg

Ingredients:

- 3 ½ c egg noodles, uncooked
- ½ tsp pepper
- 1 tsp salt
- 1 package baby spinach
- 2 c onion, chopped
- 6 c water
- 1 package mushrooms, sliced
- 4 c chicken broth
- 1 package carrot, shredded
- 1 tbsp rosemary, chopped
- ¼ c lemon juice
- 1 c celery, chopped
- 1 ½ lb boneless chicken breast, diced
- 1/3 c parsley, chopped
- 1 ½ lb boneless chicken thighs, diced
- 1 tbsp olive oil, divided

Directions:

1. Place everything in the cooker and combine. Set to slow cook for 8 hours on low.

CHAPTER 3 – POULTRY

Chinese Sweet and Sour Chicken

Total Preparation & Cook Time: 5 hours 10 minutes

Servings – 6

Nutritional info: Calories: 339, Fats: 13g, Carbs: 28g, Protein: 30g, Sugar: 26g, Sodium: 601mg

Ingredients:

- ½ c baby carrots
- container pre-chopped onion
- container pre-chopped tricolor bell pepper
- 2 lbs boneless chicken thighs
- 1 tbsp ginger, grated
- 2 tbsp cornstarch
- 3 tbsp soy sauce
- ¼ c rice vinegar
- ¼ c brown sugar
- 1 tbsp garlic, minced
- can pineapple chunks

Directions:

1. Spray your cooker with nonstick spray.
2. Reserving a cup of the pineapple juice.
3. Mix together the juice, ginger, garlic, cornstarch, soy sauce, vinegar, and sugar in the cooker. Make sure it is smooth.
4. Stir in the carrots, onion, pepper, and chicken. Make sure everything is coated.
5. Set to slow for 5-6 hours on low.
6. Once done, mix in the pineapple.

Creamy Lemon Chicken

Total Preparation & Cook Time: 6 hours 50 minutes

Servings – 6

Nutritional info: Calories: 341, Fats: 5g, Carbs: 31g, Protein: 38g, Sugar: 6g, Sodium: 327mg

Ingredients:

- 3 tbsp dill, chopped
- 12 oz artichokes
- 1 red bell pepper, sliced
- 2 tbsp arrowroot starch
- 1 tbsp olive oil
- ¼ c Greek yogurt
- ¼ c lemon juice
- ½ tsp salt
- 2 c chicken broth
- 3 garlic cloves, minced
- ½ tsp pepper
- 6 5oz boneless chicken breasts
- 6 potatoes, quartered

Directions:

1. Put the potatoes in your cooker and then add the bell pepper.

2. Coat the chicken with pepper and salt. Brown chicken in a skillet. Place the chicken on top of the bell pepper layer. Roast the garlic in the skillet and then place over top of the chicken. Pour in the broth. Set to slow cook for 6-7 hours on low.

3. Take out the chicken. Retrieve a quarter up of the liquid and pour into a bowl. Mix with the arrowroot,

yogurt, and lemon juice. Combine this mixture back into pot. Mix in the dill and artichokes. Place the chicken back in. Continue cooking for another 30 minutes.

Duck a l'Orange

Total Preparation & Cook Time: 10 hours 20 minutes

Servings – 4

Nutritional info: Calories: 155, Fats: 3g, Carbs: 15g, Protein: 12g, Sugar: 3g, Sodium: 330mg

Ingredients:

- 1 can orange juice concentrate
- 1 onion, cut in eights
- 1 apple, sliced
- 2 oranges, peeled and sliced
- ¼ tsp pepper
- ½ tsp salt
- 2 duck breasts, cut in half

Directions:

1. Season the duck with pepper and salt. Place in the duck, then oranges, then the apples, and lastly the onion. Pour the orange juice over everything.
2. Set to slow cook for 8-10 hours on low.
3. Take out the duck and discard the leftover liquid.

Duck Cassoulet

Total Preparation & Cook Time: 8 hours

Servings – 8

Nutritional info: Calories: 548, Fats: 26.8 g, Carbs: 40.2 g, Protein: 36.7 g, Sugar: 8 g, Sodium: 584mg

Ingredients:

- 1 tomato, chopped
- 1 lb duck breast halves
- 3 garlic cloves, minced
- 3 carrots, sliced
- bay leaf
- 1 lb dry navy beans, soaked
- sprig rosemary
- ½ lb bacon
- sprig thyme
- 3 sprigs parsley
- onion, peeled
- 1 tbsp whole cloves
- 1 lb pork sausage links, sliced

Directions:

1. Brown the sausage in a skillet.
2. Press the cloves in the onion. Roll up bacon and tie together with a string. Take the rosemary, parsley, and thyme and tie together.
3. In the pot, put the duck, garlic, carrots, bay leaf, herbs, clove onion, bacon, sausage, and beans. Add water to cover all ingredients. Set to slow cook. Set time to an hour on high. Lower heat to low and cook 6-8 hours.
4. Take out the herbs, onion, and bacon. Mix in the tomatoes. Cook for another half hour.

Italian Turkey

Total Preparation & Cook Time: 8 hours 35 minutes

Servings – 6

Nutritional info: Calories: 117, Fats: 1 g, Carbs: 6.1 g, Protein: 20.1 g, Sugar: 2g, Sodium: 813mg

Ingredients:

- ½ c water
- packet brown gravy mix
- 1 tbsp Worcestershire sauce
- 1 tsp oregano
- onion, chopped
- ¼ c white vinegar
- 2 garlic cloves, minced
- 1 boneless turkey breast half
- green bell pepper, sliced
- 1 quart water
- 4 beef bouillon cubes

Directions:

1. Place the bouillon in the water and let it dissolve. Place in the cooker. Put the turkey in the cooker and add water if needed to cover it.

2. Set to slow cook on low for 8-10 hours. Mix in the Worcestershire sauce, oregano, garlic, pepper, onion, and vinegar when there is two hours left.

3. Mix together the water and brown gravy. Add into the cooker and let it cook another 20 minutes.

Neapolitan Chicken Cacciatore

Total Preparation & Cook Time: 5 hours

Servings – 6

Nutritional info: Calories: 376, Fats: 10 g, Carbs: 15 g, Protein: 52 g, Sugar: 3g, Sodium: 718mg

Ingredients:

- ¼ c Romano cheese
- 1 tbsp olive oil
- 1 green bell pepper, chopped
- ½ c dry red wine
- ½ tsp pepper
- ½ tsp salt
- 1 can crushed tomatoes
- ¼ tsp crushed red pepper flakes
- 6 oz mushrooms, sliced
- 1 c chicken broth
- 1 celery stalk, chopped
- 3 garlic cloves, chopped
- 1 tbsp tomato paste
- onion, chopped
- whole chicken, skinned and chopped

Directions:

1. Sprinkle chicken with pepper and salt.
2. Brown the chicken in smalls batches in a skillet.
3. Place the mushrooms, garlic, pepper, celery, and onion in layers on your cooker.
4. Put the chicken on top of all of the veggies.

Chapter 3 – Poultry

5. Mix together the pepper flakes, tomato paste, broth, wine, and tomatoes. Pour the mixture on the chicken.//
6. Take out the chicken.
7. Thicken the sauce with a flour slurry and drizzle over chicken.

Paprika Chicken

Total Preparation & Cook Time: 6 hours

Servings – 6

Nutritional info: Calories: 270, Fats: 13 g, Carbs: 28 g, Protein: 13 g, Sugar: 1g, Sodium: 556mg

Ingredients:

- 2 tbsp parsley, chopped
- 3 chicken quarters
- 1 c chicken broth
- 1 tsp salt
- 8 lemon slices
- 1 ½ tbsp capers
- 1 tbsp olive oil
- 6 potatoes, halved
- 2 tsp garlic powder
- 2 tbsp smoked paprika

Directions:

1. Half the chicken quarters. Make sure to trim off excess fat, leave on the skin.
2. Combine garlic powder, 1 tsp salt, and paprika. Season chicken and potatoes in this mixture.
3. Brown the chicken in a skillet for a few minutes.
4. Place the potatoes and chicken in the cooker. Mix in the broth, lemon, and capers. Combine everything well.
5. Set to slow cook for 4-6 hours on high.
6. Serve with parsley and more lemon.

Salsa Chicken

Total Preparation & Cook Time: 6 hours 20 minutes

Servings – 8

Nutritional info: Calories: 148, Fats: 2.4 g, Carbs: 7.5 g, Protein: 23.1 g, Sugar: 0g, Sodium: 540mg

Ingredients:

- ¼ c water
- 1 c salsa
- ½ c carrot, shredded
- ½ c celery, chopped
- 1 c diced tomatoes with habaneros
- 2 tbsp taco seasoning
- 1 c onion, chopped
- 2 lbs boneless chicken

Directions:

1. Place chicken on the bottom on the pot. Season with the taco seasoning. Place in the carrot, celery, onion, and tomatoes. Pour in the salsa. Add in the water.
2. Set to slow cook for 6-8 hours on low. Chicken should reach 165 degrees.
3. Remove chicken and shred with forks. Mix back into the salsa.

Spicy Chicken

Total Preparation & Cook Time: 4 hours 15 minutes

Servings – 3

Nutritional info: Calories: 152, Fats: 2.8 g, Carbs: 7.1 g, Protein: 24.4 g, Sugar: 0g, Sodium: 392mg

Ingredients:

- pinch salt
- 2 garlic cloves, minced
- pinch pepper
- 1 tsp cumin
- onion, chopped
- 1 tsp chili powder
- ¼ c tomato sauce
- ½ jar salsa
- 3 boneless chicken breasts

Directions:

1. Put your chicken in your pot. Top with tomato sauce and salsa. Mix in the pepper, salt, chili powder, cumin, onion, and garlic. Set to slow cook for 4-5 hours on low.
2. Remove chicken and shred then mix back into mixture.

Thanksgiving Turkey

Total Preparation & Cook Time: 8 hours 15 minutes

Servings – 12

Nutritional info: Calories: 382, Fats: 15.6 g, Carbs: 2.6 g, Protein: 54.2 g, Sugar: 0g, Sodium: 379mg

Ingredients:

- 1 tsp dried sage
- 2 tbsp AP flour
- 1 can turkey gravy
- 1 tbsp Worcestershire sauce
- ½ tsp garlic pepper
- 1 bone in turkey breast
- 5 slices bacon

Directions:

1. Cooke the bacon in a skillet until crispy and then crumble.
2. Coat your cooker with nonstick spray. Put the turkey in the pot. Sprinkle over with garlic. Combine the sage, Worcestershire, flour, gravy, and bacon together. Place this mixture on the turkey.
3. Set to slow cook on low for 8 hours.

Turkey Legs

Total Preparation & Cook Time: 7 hours 10 minutes

Servings – 12

Nutritional info: Calories: 217, Fats: 6.9 g, Carbs: .2 g, Protein: 36.3 g, Sugar: 0g, Sodium: 102mg

Ingredients:

- 6 12 by 16 inch foil squares
- pepper
- salt
- 3 tsp poultry seasoning, divided
- 6 turkey legs

Directions:

1. Clean off the legs and dry. Season the legs with pepper, salt, and ½ tsp of poultry seasoning. Wrap each leg with foil when seasoned.
2. Put the legs in the cooker with nothing else. Set to slow cook for 7-8 hours on low.

Chapter 3 – Poultry

Turkey Sausage Cassoulet

Total Preparation & Cook Time: 7 hours

Servings – 6

Nutritional info: Calories: 382, Fats: 19 g, Carbs: 25 g, Protein: 27 g, Sugar: 8g, Sodium: 902mg

Ingredients:

- ½ c precooked bacon crumbles
- 2 cans northern beans, drained
- 1 tsp pepper
- 2 tsp herbes de Provence
- 1 can tomato sauce
- 1 ¼ lbs Italian turkey sausage, sliced
- 2 tbsp minced garlic
- ¼ c olive oil
- ¾ c baby carrots, halved
- 1 c onion, chopped

Directions:

1. Combine the garlic, oil, carrots, and onion in a heat sage dish. Top with saran wrap except for one corner
2. Microwave for 4 minutes.
3. Spray your cooker with nonstick spray.
4. Mix the pepper, herbes, tomato sauce, sausage, and onion mixture in the cooker. Mix well.
5. Set to slow cook for 7-8 hours on low.
6. During the last hour mix in the beans.

7. Cook the bacon in the microwave and sprinkle over dish when ready to serve.

CHAPTER 4 – BEEF, PORK & LAMB

Barbecue Pulled Pork

Total Preparation & Cook Time: 5 hours 30 minutes

Servings – 8

Nutritional info: Calories: 214, Fats: 8 g, Carbs: 9 g, Protein: 25 g, Sugar: 6g, Sodium: 321mg

Ingredients:

- 1 garlic clove, minced
- 2 ½ lb Boston butt
- 4 oz can chopped green chilies
- ½ tsp salt
- 2 tbsp honey
- 1 tbsp tomato paste
- onion, chopped
- 3 tbsp ACV
- 1 tbsp Worcestershire sauce
- 8 oz can tomato sauce
- 1 tbsp smoked paprika
- 2 tsp dry mustard
- 1 tsp ground chipotle

Directions:

1. Mix together the salt, chipotle, mustard, Worcestershire, tomato paste, paprika, honey, vinegar, chilies, and tomato sauce in your cooker. Mix in the garlic, pork, and onion. Combine well.

2. Set to slow cook. Set to low for five hours

3. Remove the pork and shred. Place back in the sauce and mix everything together

Bolognese

Total Preparation & Cook Time: 6 hours 20 minutes

Servings – 20

Nutritional info: Calories: 143, Fats: 7 g, Carbs: 5 g, Protein: 15 g, Sugar: 3g, Sodium: 145mg

Ingredients:

- ½ c half and half
- ¼ c parsley
- salt
- pepper
- 3 bay leaves
- 2 cans crushed tomatoes
- ¼ c white wine
- 2 lbs ground beef
- 2 carrots, minced
- 2 celery stalks, minced
- large onion, minced
- 1 tbsp butter
- 4 oz pancetta, chopped

Directions:

1. Cook the pancetta in a skillet. Mix in carrots, celery, onions, and butter. Cook until everything is soft.

2. Place meat, pepper, and salt to skillet and brown. Remove the fat and add the wine. Reduce it a little.

3. Pour mixture into the cooker along with more pepper, salt, bay leaves, and tomatoes. Set to slow cook for 6 hours on low.

4. Check your seasoning and add more if needed. Mix in parsley and half and half. Serve with pasta.

Braised Beef Ragu

Total Preparation & Cook Time: 8 hours 20 minutes

Servings – 10

Nutritional info: Calories: 461, Fats: 23.4 g, Carbs: 28.8 g, Protein: 31.5 g, Sugar: 4.3g, Sodium: 1009mg

Ingredients:

- pepper
- 2 tsp salt
- 2 bay leaves
- 3 tbsp tomato paste
- 2 tbsp olive oil
- ½ c red wine
- 1 tsp oregano
- 2 cans whole tomatoes
- 1 tsp basil
- 3 garlic cloves, minced
- ½ onion, minced
- 3 lbs beef rump roast

Directions:

1. Put everything in the pot. Set to slow cook for 7-8 hours on low. Remove beef and shred. Stir beef back into the mixture.
2. Serve over polenta.

Coffee Braised Pot Roast

Total Preparation & Cook Time: 8 hours 15 minutes

Servings – 10

Nutritional info: Calories: 209, Fats: 7 g, Carbs: 4g, Protein: 30 g, Sugar: 2g, Sodium: 73mg

Ingredients:

- 2 onions, sliced
- 2 tbsp cornstarch combined with 2 tbsp water
- ¾ c strong coffee
- 1 tsp thyme
- 4 garlic cloves, minced
- pepper
- 4 tsp EVOO, divided
- 2 tbsp balsamic vinegar
- ½ tsp salt
- 4 lb beef chuck roast, trimmed

Directions:

1. Sprinkle pepper and salt over the beef and brown it in a skillet. Place the brown beef in your cooker.

2. Cook your onions until they are golden. Mix in the thyme and garlic. Pour in the vinegar and coffee and let simmer for a few minutes. Pour mixture over the beef in the cooker.

3. Set to slow cook. Set to low for seven to eight hours, or low for four and a half to five hours.

4. Remove beef and let rest 10 minutes. Mix in the cornstarch to the liquid mixture and let thicken. Serve gravy over the beef.

Chapter 4 – Beef, Pork & Lamb

Lamb Ribs

Total Preparation & Cook Time: 10 hours 10 minutes

Servings – 4

Nutritional info: Calories: 371.5, Fats: 31.8 g, Carbs: 2g, Protein: 18.4 g, Sugar: 0g, Sodium: 339.6mg

Ingredients:

- 1 tsp EVOO olive oil
- pepper
- salt
- sprinkle thyme
- 5 garlic cloves, minced
- 1 lb lamb spare ribs

Directions:

1. Place the ribs in the pot.
2. Place the other ingredients on top.
3. Set to slow cook for 1-2 hours on high. Turn heat down to low and 8 more hours.

Leg Of Lamb

Total Preparation & Cook Time: 10 hours 5 minutes

Servings – 20

Nutritional info: Calories: 158, Fats: 5.9 g, Carbs: 3 g, Protein: 22 g, Sugar: 0g, Sodium: 727.7mg

Ingredients:

- onion, sliced
- 5 c water
- 1 pkt onion soup mix
- 2 garlic cloves, minced
- ½ c soy sauce
- 4 lbs leg of lamb, rolled

Directions:

1. Put everything in the cooker and mix. Set to slow cook for 8-10 hours on low. Take out lamb and allow it to rest a few minutes before slicing.

Moroccan Lamb Tagine

Total Preparation & Cook Time: 8 hours 40 minutes

Servings – 6

Nutritional info: Calories: 420.6, Fats: 13 g, Carbs: 56.4 g Protein: 25 g, Sugar: 0g, Sodium: 955.1mg

Ingredients:

- 1 tbsp water
- 1 tbsp sun dried tomato past
- 1 can chicken broth
- 1 can chickpeas
- ¾ c dried prunes, chopped
- ¾ c dried apricots, chopped
- lemon zest
- 1 tbsp cornstarch
- 1tbsp ginger, grated
- 3 garlic cloves
- ½ tsp ground ginger
- 1 tsp salt
- 1 eggplant
- 5 carrots, diced
- 1 tsp cinnamon
- 2 onions, cubed
- ½ tsp ground cardamom
- 1 tbsp honey
- ¾ tsp ground coriander
- ¾ tsp garlic powder
- ¼ tsp turmeric
- 2 tsp paprika
- ¼ tsp cayenne
- 3 tbsp oil
- ½ tsp cumin
- ¼ tsp ground cloves
- 1 ½ lb lamb, cubed

Directions:

1. Heat oil in a skillet and cook the lamb until browned. Mix in the spices and cook until fragrant. Place the lamb in the cooker.

2. Heat more oil and cook the ginger, garlic, eggplant, carrots, and onion for a couple of minutes. Then mix the remaining ingredients.

3. Place everything in the cooker. Set to slow cook for 8 hours on low.

Pork Roast

Total Preparation & Cook Time: 10 hours 45 minutes

Servings – 8

Nutritional info: Calories: 227, Fats: 6 g, Carbs: 11 g, Protein: 31g, Sugar: 0g, Sodium: 390mg

Ingredients:

- ½ c chicken broth
- 1 tsp sesame oil
- 2 lb boneless pork shoulder
- 2 tsp garlic, minced
- 3 tbsp ketchup
- ½ tsp five spice powder
- 2 tsp ginger, grated
- 3 tbsp honey
- ¼ c hoisin sauce
- ¼ c soy sauce

Directions:

1. Mix the last 8 ingredients together. Place the pork in a baggie and top with mixture. Let it marinate for 2 hours. Flip occasionally to evenly coat.
2. Pour marinade and pork in the cooker. Set to slow cook for 8 hours on low.
3. Take the pork out and tent with foil and let rest.
4. Mix the broth into the pot. Let it cook with the rest of the liquid for 30 minutes on low.
5. Shred the pork and drizzle with the sauce to serve.

Red Curry Bison Short Ribs

Total Preparation & Cook Time: 8 hours 50 minutes

Servings – 6

Nutritional info: Calories: 20, Fats: 4 g, Carbs: 11 g, Protein: 31 g, Sugar: 5g, Sodium: 869mg

Ingredients:

- pepper
- 6 bok choy, halved
- 1 c coconut milk
- 3 tomatoes, diced
- 2 tbsp lime juice
- 3 tbsp fish sauce
- 1 ½ c chicken broth
- 2 c onion, sliced
- 3 lb bone in bison short ribs
- 2 tsp oil
- ½ c water
- 6 scallions, chopped
- ½ c cilantro, chopped
- 3 slices of ginger
- 3 garlic cloves, peeled
- 1 ½ tsp red curry paste

Directions:

1. Put the water, scallions, cilantro, ginger, garlic, and curry paste in a food processor. Mix them until they create a paste, adding more water if you need it.
2. Heat a skillet with oil and brown the ribs.

3. Place the lime juice, fish sauce, broth, onion, and curry in the cooker and mix together. Add in the ribs. Set to slow cook for 8 hours on low.

4. Remove ribs. Mix in the coconut milk and tomatoes. Stir in the bok choy. Let cook 20 minutes on high. Season with more lime juice and pepper if needed.

Red Curry Pulled Pork

Total Preparation & Cook Time: 4 hours

Servings – 10

Nutritional info: Calories: 456, Fats: 19 g, Carbs: 46 g, Protein: 31g, Sugar: 7g, Sodium: 728mg

Ingredients:

- salt
- 4 tsp oil
- 2 tbsp + 2 tsp lime juice
- ¼ c cilantro, chopped
- 1 c carrot, shredded
- 2 c cabbage, sliced
- lime zest
- ¼ c coconut milk
- 2 baguettes
- 3 ½ lb boneless pork shoulder
- 1 ½ tbsp fish sauce
- ¼ c thai red curry paste, divided
- ¼ c lime juice
- ¼ c brown sugar, packed

Directions:

1. Mix together fish sauce, 3 tbsp curry paste, ¼ c lime juice, and brown sugar in the cooker. Place in the pork and coat in mixture. Set to slow cook for 4 hours on high, or 8 hours on low.
2. Remove the pork.
3. For the slaw, mix together the salt, oil, lime juice, cilantro, carrot, and cabbage.

Chapter 4 – Beef, Pork & Lamb

4. Cut baguettes in 5 pieces. Toast them if you want. Take the pork and shred it. Mix it back into the sauce along with 1 tbsp curry paste, lime zest, and coconut milk. Mix well.

5. Place on the baguette along with the slaw.

Rosemary Lamb

Total Preparation & Cook Time: 8 hours 15 minutes

Servings – 8

Nutritional info: Calories: 264.5, Fats: 8.6 g, Carbs: 25.3 g, Protein: 21.5 g, Sugar: 0g, Sodium: 551.5mg

Ingredients:

- 2 tbsp butter, melted
- 1 tsp pepper
- ¼ tsp oregano
- ½ tbsp garlic, minced
- 1 tsp paprika
- 3 tsp Worcestershire sauce
- 1 lb baby carrots
- 1 lb onions, quartered
- 1 tbsp rosemary
- 1.5 lb potatoes, quartered
- 1.5 lb lamb, cubed
- 4 c beef broth

Directions:

1. Place the following ingredients in cooker as such: broth, potato, onion, carrot, lamb.
2. Drizzle with Worcestershire, and sprinkle over with the spices.
3. Pour the melted butter over everything.
4. Set to slow cook for 8 hours on low.

Chapter 4 – Beef, Pork & Lamb

Sweet Tangy Short Ribs

Total Preparation & Cook Time: 8 hours 58 minutes

Servings – 8

Nutritional info: Calories: 234, Fats: 11.6 g, Carbs: 16.5 g, Protein: 15.4g, Sugar: 0g, Sodium: 533mg

Ingredients:

- ¼ c cilantro
- 2 c snow peas
- 1 tbsp cornstarch
- 2 tbsp sambal oelek
- ¼ c water
- 4 c carrot
- strip orange rind
- star anise
- 2 tbsp ginger, grated
- can cola
- 8 garlic cloves, minced
- 1/3 c soy sauce
- 2 tbsp brown sugar
- ¼ c rice vinegar
- ¾ c beef stock
- 8 bone in beef short ribs
- 2 tbsp oil, divided

Directions:

1. Heat a skillet with oil and brown the ribs. Put the ribs in the cooker. Mix in the stock, soy sauce, vinegar, ginger, sugar, oelek, garlic, cola, anise, and orange rind. Set to slow cook for 8 hours on low. Remove the ribs. Get rid of the rind and star anise.

2. Remove the fat floating on top. Mix in the carrot. Cook on high 20 minutes. Mix the cornstarch with ¼ c water,

and mix into the liquid. Allow liquid to thicken and then stir in the peas.

3. Serve ribs with the sauce.

CHAPTER 5 – VEGETARIAN & VEGAN

Barley Chickpea Risotto

Total Preparation & Cook Time: 3 hours

Servings – 8

Nutritional info: Calories: 266, Fats: 4.7 g, Carbs: 45.9 g, Protein: 12.1 g, Sugar: 6.4g, Sodium: 303mg

Ingredients:

- 3 tbsp parsley, chopped
- 1/3 c parmesan
- ½ tsp salt
- 1 ¼ c water
- 2 ½ c vegetable broth
- 3 carrots, chopped
- 1 ½ tbsp lemon juice
- 1 can garbanzo beans, rinsed
- ½ head cauliflower, chopped
- 1 ¼ c pearl barley
- 4 thyme sprigs
- ½ onion, minced
- ¼ tsp pepper
- 3 garlic cloves, minced
- 1 ½ tbsp EVOO

Directions:

1. Heat skillet with oil and place in onion, cauliflower, garlic, and carrots. Let the vegetables cook until soft.
2. Mix in the barley and thyme.

3. Place the veggie mixture in your cooker. Mix in the pepper, salt, water, broth, and beans. Set to slow cook for 2-2 ½ hours on high. All liquid should be absorbed.

4. Takeout the thyme sprigs. Mix in the lemon juice.

Chapter 5 – Vegetarian & Vegan

Eggplant Parmesan

Total Preparation & Cook Time: 5 hours 30 minutes

Servings – 8

Nutritional info: Calories: 401, Fats: 18.3 g, Carbs: 38.6 g, Protein: 23 g, Sugar: 0g, Sodium: 1870mg

Ingredients:

- package mozzarella, sliced
- 2 eggs
- 32 oz jar marinara sauce
- ½ c parmesan, grated
- 3 tbsp AP flour
- 1/3 c water
- 4 eggplant, peeled and sliced
- 1 tbsp salt
- 1/3 c breadcrumbs, seasoned
- 1 c EVOO olive oil

Directions:

1. Layer the eggplant slices in a bowl. Season every layer with salt. Let the eggplant sit for 30 minutes. Drain and rinse the eggplant.
2. Heat some oil in a pan. Mix together the flour, water, and eggs. Coat the eggplant in the egg mixture and brown both sides in the skillet.
3. Mix the parmesan and breadcrumbs together. Put a layer of eggplant in your cooker. Sprinkle with breadcrumbs. Pour on some marinara and sprinkle with mozzarella. Continue layering this way until all ingredients are used.
4. Set to slow cook for 4-5 hour on low.

Picadillo Stuffed Peppers

Total Preparation & Cook Time: 8 hours 25 minutes

Servings – 4

Nutritional info: Calories: 325, Fats: 7 g, Carbs: 51 g, Protein: 18 g, Sugar: 11g, Sodium: 800mg

Ingredients:

- ¼ c raisins
- 1/3 c onion, chopped
- 2 c rice, cooked
- ½ bell peppers
- 4 large bell peppers
- ¼ tsp cinnamon
- 1 tsp cumin
- 1 tbsp red wine vinegar
- 26 oz jar marinara sauce

Directions:

1. Mix together the cinnamon, cumin, vinegar, and marinara sauce.
2. Place 1 1/3 cups of this mixture in the bottom of your cooker.
3. Chop up the bell pepper half.
4. Cut off the top of the other peppers, and remove their seeds.
5. Mix together the remaining sauce, chopped pepper, raisins, onion, and rice.
6. Place this mixture inside of the pepper and place their tops back on them.

Chapter 5 – Vegetarian & Vegan

7. Put the peppers in the cooker. Set to slow cook. Set to low for six to eight hours.

8. Serve with the sauce and parsley.

Pinto Bean Sloppy Joe

Total Preparation & Cook Time: 5 hours 30 minutes

Servings – 10

Nutritional info: Calories: 281, Fats: 6 g, Carbs: 50 g, Protein: 11 g, Sugar: 13g, Sodium: 721mg

Ingredients:

- 10 hamburger buns
- 1 onion, sliced
- 1 tsp salt
- 3 tbsp honey mustard
- 1 zucchini, chopped
- 4 c cabbage
- 2 tbsp soy sauce
- 8oz can tomato sauce
- 1 tbsp brown sugar
- 2 carrots, sliced
- 1 c corn
- 1 bell pepper, diced
- 1 c dry pinto beans, soaked
- 2 tbsp EVOO
- ½ c water
- 2 tbsp tomato paste
- 2 tbsp balsamic vinegar
- 3 tbsp chili powder
- 4 garlic cloves, minced

Directions:

1. Cook onion and carrots in a skillet until browned. Mix in the chili powder and garlic. Take off the heat and mix in the vinegar to deglaze the pan.

Chapter 5 – Vegetarian & Vegan

2. Coat your cooker with nonstick spray. Place beans in the pot. Mix in the tomato paste, soy sauce, water, tomato sauce, and pepper. Sprinkle the onion mixture on top. Don't mix together. Set to slow cook. Set time to 5 hours when cooking on high, or 9 hours when cooking on low.

3. Mix in the salt, sugar, mustard, corn, zucchini, and cabbage. Set for 30 minutes on high.

4. Place mixture on buns and serve.

Quinoa Black Bean Peppers

Total Preparation & Cook Time: 6 hours 25 minutes

Servings – 6

Nutritional info: Calories: 434, Fats: 12.9 g, Carbs: 59.5 g, Protein: 22.7 g, Sugar: 6.2g, Sodium: 318mg

Ingredients:

- 1 ½ c pepper jack cheese, shredded
- ½ tsp garlic salt
- 1 c quinoa, rinsed
- 1 tsp cumin
- 14 oz can refried beans
- 14 oz can black beans, rinsed
- 1 tsp onion powder
- 1 tsp chili powder
- 6 bell peppers
- 1 ½ c red enchilada sauce

Directions:

1. Remove the tops for the peppers and take out the seeds and ribs.
2. Mix together 1 cup of cheese, spices, enchilada sauce, beans, and quinoa. Spoon the mixture into each pepper.
3. Place a half a cup of water in the cooker. Set the peppers in the water. Set to slow cook. Set for six hours; low, or three hours; high. Sprinkle the rest of the cheese over the peppers.
4. Top with desired toppings such as sour cream, avocado, or cilantro.

Root Vegetable Tagine

Total Preparation & Cook Time: 9 hours 50 minutes

Servings – 8

Nutritional info: Calories: 131, Fats: .7 g, Carbs: 31 g, Protein: 2.8 g, Sugar: 0g, Sodium: 187mg

Ingredients:

- 14oz can vegetable broth
- 1 tbsp cilantro
- ½ tsp ginger
- 1 tbsp parsley
- ¼ tsp cayenne
- 1 lb turnips, diced
- ½ tsp cinnamon
- 1 tsp cumin
- 4 prunes, chopped
- 6 dried apricots, chopped
- 1 lb carrots, diced
- 1 tsp turmeric
- 2 onions, chopped
- 1 lb parsnips, diced

Directions:

1. Place all of the ingredient into your cooker and stir well to combine.
2. Set to slow cook on low for 9 hours.

Sweet Potato

Total Preparation & Cook Time: 4 hours 10 minutes

Servings – 4

Nutritional info: Calories: 186, Fats: 6.5 g, Carbs: 31 g, Protein: 2 g, Sugar: 9g, Sodium: 97mg

Ingredients:

- 1 tbsp oil
- ¼ tsp nutmeg
- 1 tbsp honey
- 1 tsp cinnamon
- 3 tbsp water
- 1 tbsp butter, melted
- 4 sweet potatoes

Directions:

1. Clean off the potatoes and poke with a fork several times.
2. Mix together the nutmeg, cinnamon, water, honey, butter, and oil.
3. Rub the potatoes in the mixture.
4. Put the potatoes in the cooker.
5. Sprinkle with pepper and salt.
6. Set slow cook for 4-6 hours on low.

Chapter 5 – Vegetarian & Vegan

Vegan Jambalaya

Total Preparation & Cook Time: 4 hours 55 minutes

Servings – 6

Nutritional info: Calories: 334, Fats: 10.3 g, Carbs: 40.8 g, Protein: 19.9 g, Sugar: 0g, Sodium: 965mg

Ingredients:

- 1 c rice
- ½ tsp oregano
- ½ large green bell pepper, chopped
- 1 ½ tsp Cajun seasoning
- 1 tbsp miso paste
- 2 garlic cloves, minced
- 1 c vegetable broth
- 3 celery stalks, chopped
- ½ onion, chopped
- 8 oz smoked vegan sausage, sliced
- 8 oz seitan, cubed
- 28 oz diced tomatoes
- 1 tbsp oil

Directions:

1. Drizzle the oil on the bottom of your cooker. Mix together everything, except the rice, in the pot.

2. Set to slow cook for 4 hours on low. Mix in the rice. Turn temp to high for 30 minutes, or until rice is cooked.

Vegetable Curry

Total Preparation & Cook Time: 8 hours

Servings – 6

Nutritional info: Calories: 161, Fats: 5 g, Carbs: 24 g, Protein: 7g, Sugar: 8g, Sodium: 373mg

Ingredients:

- 1 c peas
- 8 oz green beans
- 1 large red bell pepper, sliced
- 8 oz cauliflower florets
- 2 onions, sliced
- 2 potatoes, chunked
- ½ tsp salt
- 2 ½ tbsp curry paste
- ¼ c AP flour
- 14 oz coconut milk

Directions:

1. Mix together the salt, curry paste, flour, and milk in your cooker until smooth.
2. Mix in the pepper, cauliflower, onions, and potatoes.
3. Pour the beans over top of everything.
4. Set to slow cook for 6-8hours on low. The veggies should be tender.
5. Mix in the cilantro and peas.

Chapter 5 – Vegetarian & Vegan

Vegetable Pot Pie

Total Preparation & Cook Time: 5 hours

Servings – 8

Nutritional info: Calories: 346, Fats: 12.7 g, Carbs: 48.2 g, Protein: 11.9 g, Sugar: 0g, Sodium: 606mg

Ingredients:

Biscuit

- 1 c buttermilk
- ¾ tsp baking soda
- 3 tbsp chives, chopped
- 1/8 tsp salt
- oz AP flour
- 1 ½ tsp baking powder
- 2 oz parmesan, grated
- 4 ½ tbsp butter
- 1 tsp pepper

Filling

- 16 oz pearl onions
- 1 ½ tbsp thyme
- 2 c petite green peas
- ¾ c vegetable broth
- 1 ½ c milk
- 2 ½ tbsp AP flour
- cooking spray
- 1 ¼ c carrot, diced
- 2 garlic cloves, minced
- ½ tsp pepper
- ¼ tsp salt
- 2 packages pre-sliced mushrooms
- ¾ c celery, chopped
- 1 c parsnip, diced
- 2 c potato, diced

- 2 tbsp oil, divided

Directions:

1. Heat a skillet with oil. Mix in the potato, carrot, parsnip, celery, mushrooms, salt, and pepper. Cook until soft. Mix in the garlic. Spray your cooker with nonstick spray. Place the veggies in the cooker.

2. Place 1 ½ tbsp of oil in the skillet and mix in 2 ½ tbsp flour. Whisk in the broth and milk. Cook until it starts to become thick. Pour over the veggies. Mix in the onions, thyme, and peas. Set to slow cook for 3 ½ hours on low.

3. Topping: Mix together the dry ingredients for the biscuits. Using knives or pastry cutter, cut in the butter. This mix should look like cornmeal. Mix in the chives and cheese. Mix in the buttermilk.

4. Set the heat to high. Place drops of the topping onto the filling. Cook for another 1 and 15 minutes.

Chapter 5 – Vegetarian & Vegan

Vegetarian Curry

Total Preparation & Cook Time: 9 hours 25 minutes

Servings – 4

Nutritional info: Calories: 407, Fats: 3 g, Carbs: 87 g, Protein: 13 g, Sugar: 0g, Sodium: 1068mg

Ingredients:

- cooked rice
- 14 ½ oz diced tomatoes
- 2 tbsp quick cooking tapioca
- ¼ tsp crushed red pepper
- 14 oz vegetable broth
- 1/8 tsp cinnamon
- 1 tsp ground coriander
- 3 garlic cloves, minced
- 2 tsp curry powder
- 8 oz green beans
- 15 oz can garbanzo beans
- ¼ tsp salt
- 2 potatoes, cubed
- 4 carrots, sliced
- 1 c onion, chopped

Directions:

1. In your cooker mix together the cinnamon, salt, red pepper, coriander, curry powder, tapioca, garlic, onion, green beans, garbanzo beans, potatoes, and carrots. Add in the broth.

2. Set to slow cook. Let it cook for seven to nine hours on low, or three and a half to four and a half hours on high.

3. Mix in the tomatoes. Let it sit for a few minutes and serve with rice.

Vegetarian Lasagna

Total Preparation & Cook Time: 2 hours

Servings – 8

Nutritional info: Calories: 413, Fats: 14 g, Carbs: 49 g, Protein: 27 g, Sugar: 9g, Sodium: 665mg

Ingredients:

- 3 c mozzarella, divided
- 3 garlic cloves, minced
- 15 lasagna noodles, uncooked
- 3 large Portobello mushroom caps
- pinch crushed red pepper
- 1 zucchini, quartered
- 28 oz crushed tomatoes
- 5 oz package baby spinach
- 28 oz can diced tomato
- 15 oz container ricotta
- egg

Directions:

1. Mix together the zucchini, mushrooms, spinach, ricotta, and egg.
2. Mix together red pepper, garlic, and both tomatoes in a separate bowl.
3. Coat your cooker with nonstick spray. Put 1 ½ cups of tomato in the pot. Place noodles on top. Spoon in the

veggie mixture. Place 1 ½ cup of sauce and sprinkle with mozzarella. Start another layer with noodles. Continue until you run out of ingredients. It should end with the tomato sauce.

4. Set to slow cook. Let cook two hours on high, or four hours on low. Top with the remaining mozzarella. Let the cheese melt for 10 minutes.

CHAPTER 6 – PASTA & GRAINS

Baked Spaghetti

Total Preparation & Cook Time: 3 hours 25 minutes

Servings – 8

Nutritional info: Calories: 234, Fats: 10 g, Carbs: 43 g, Protein: 9g, Sugar: 1g, Sodium: 230mg

Ingredients:

- ½ c parmesan
- 1 tbsp oil
- 4 oz fontina cheese
- 8 oz mozzarella
- 24 oz jar fire roasted tomato sauce
- 2 tsp garlic, minced
- 8 oz pre-chopped onion/bell pepper mix
- 1 lb Italian sausage
- 8 oz spaghetti

Directions:

1. Coat your cooker with nonstick spray.
2. Place the noodles in the bottom of the cooker and lay the rest of the ingredients, except the cheeses, on top.
3. Mix the cheeses together and springs on top. Set to slow cook for 3 hours on low. Allow to stand for 10 minutes.

Chapter 5 – Vegetarian & Vegan

Cheesy Noodle Casserole

Total Preparation & Cook Time: 8 hours 45 minutes

Servings – 6

Nutritional info: Calories: 316, Fats: 8 g, Carbs: 42 g, Protein: 17g, Sugar: 0g, Sodium: 447mg

Ingredients:

- ½ c cheddar cheese
- 16 oz extra firm tofu
- 1 ½ tsp Italian seasoning
- 1 c onion, chopped
- 8 oz extra wide noodles
- ¼ tsp pepper
- 1 c carrots, sliced
- ¼ tsp salt
- 10 ¾ oz cream of mushroom soup
- 1 c celery, sliced
- 14 ½ oz diced tomatoes
- 2 ½ c water
- 2 garlic cloves, minced

Directions:

1. In your cooker mix together the soup and water. Mix in pepper, salt, garlic, Italian seasoning, onion, carrots, celery, and tomatoes.

2. Set to slow cook. Let cook seven to eight hours on low, or three and a half to four hours on high.

3. Mix in the noodles and set to high for another 30 minutes. Mix in the tofu and serve with cheese.

Eggplant Ziti

Total Preparation & Cook Time: 8 hours 10 minutes

Servings – 6

Nutritional info: Calories: 255, Fats: 5 g, Carbs: 38 g, Protein: 14g, Sugar: 7g, Sodium: 479mg

Ingredients:

- basil
- 1 c mozzarella
- 2 garlic cloves, minced
- ½ c basil
- 8 oz ziti pasta
- ½ c water
- 1 tsp Italian seasoning
- 2 tbsp tomato paste
- ¼ c dry white wine
- 14 ½ oz crushed fire roasted tomatoes
- 2 fennel bulbs, sliced
- 4 c eggplant, chopped
- 4 oz Italian sausage

Directions:

1. Brown up the sausage, breaking it into smaller pieces as it cooks.

2. In your cooker mix together the Italian seasoning, garlic, tomato paste, wine, water, tomatoes, fennel, eggplant, and sausage. Set to slow cook. Let cook six to seven hours on low, or three to three and a half hours on high.

Chapter 6 – Pasta & Grains

3. Mix in ½ c basil. Cook on high for another 30 minutes. Top with the cheese.

Hungarian Beef Goulash

Total Preparation & Cook Time: 4 hours 30 minutes

Servings – 8

Nutritional info: Calories: 168, Fats: 5 g, Carbs: 6 g, Protein: 23g, Sugar: 3g, Sodium: 338mg

Ingredients:

- 2 tbsp parsley
- 1 tbsp cornstarch mixed in 2 tbsp water
- 14 oz beef broth
- 2 lb beef stew meat, cubed
- 14 oz diced tomatoes
- 2 bay leaves
- 2 tsp caraway seeds
- pepper
- 1 tsp Worcestershire sauce
- ¼ tsp salt
- 2 tbsp paprika
- 1 red bell pepper, chopped
- 1 large onion, chopped
- 3 garlic cloves, minced

Directions:

1. Put the beef in your cooker. Smash you caraway seeds then mix them with the pepper, salt, and paprika. Place on beef and mix. Lay bell pepper and onion on top.

2. Mix together garlic, Worcestershire sauce, broth, and tomatoes. Pour on the veggies and beef. Throw in the bay leaves.

Chapter 6 – Pasta & Grains

3. Set to slow cook for 4-4 ½ hours on high, or 7-7 ½ hours on low.

4. Take out the bay leaves. Mix in the cornstarch. Have mixture thicken.

Macaroni and Cheese

Total Preparation & Cook Time: 3 hours 10 minutes

Servings – 9

Nutritional info: Calories:272.5, Fats: 12.6 g, Carbs: 22.9 g, Protein: 16.4g, Sugar: 5.1g, Sodium: 598.2mg

Ingredients:

- 2 c cheddar cheese
- 8 oz Velveeta, cubed
- 1 tbsp butter, melted
- 1/3 c egg substitutes
- 1 ½ c milk
- 12 oz evaporated milk
- 2 c elbow macaroni

Directions:

1. Cook the macaroni as normal, but don't cook completely. Place the pasta in the cooker along with 1 ½ cups cheddar cheese, butter, egg substitute, milk, evaporate milk, and Velveeta. Mix well together.
2. Set to slow cook for 2 ¾-3 hours on low. Top with the rest of the cheddar.

Chapter 6 – Pasta & Grains

Provincial Chicken

Total Preparation & Cook Time: 8 hours 10 minutes

Servings – 6

Nutritional info: Calories: 358, Fats: 12 g, Carbs: 23 g, Protein: 8g, Sugar: 1g, Sodium: 533mg

Ingredients:

- bowtie pasta
- ½ c sour cream
- 1 c cheddar cheese
- 1 tsp basil
- 2 tbsp parsley
- 1 tbsp dried onion, minced
- 2 tbsp balsamic vinegar
- can cream of chicken soup
- 2 zucchini, diced
- 2 cans diced tomatoes
- 4 boneless chicken breasts

Directions:

1. Mix together the herbs, onion, vinegar, soup, zucchini, tomatoes, chicken, and pasta in the cooker. Set to slow cook for 6-8 hours on low.

2. Take out the chicken and dice. Place back in the cooker with the sour cream and cheese. Mix everything together and cook for another 15 minutes.

Quinoa and Sausage

Total Preparation & Cook Time: 8 hours 25 minutes

Servings – 8

Nutritional info: Calories: 279, Fats: 11 g, Carbs: 22 g, Protein: 23g, Sugar: 4g, Sodium: 772mg

Ingredients:

- 1 c cheddar cheese
- 2 packages Italian chicken sausage links
- onion, cut into wedges
- 3 sweet peppers, diced
- 2 tsp honey
- 2 tbsp stone ground mustard
- ¼ c cider vinegar
- 1 c quinoa
- can chicken broth

Directions:

1. In your cooker mix together the honey, mustard, vinegar, quinoa, and broth. Stir in the sausage, sweet peppers, and onions.
2. Set to slow cook. Let cook four to five hours on low, or 2-2 ½ hours on high.
3. Top with cheese.

Chapter 6 – Pasta & Grains

Quinoa Casserole

Total Preparation & Cook Time: 4 hours

Servings – 10

Nutritional info: Calories: 111, Fats: 3 g, Carbs: 18 g, Protein: 5g, Sugar: 6g, Sodium: 286mg

Ingredients:

- 2 tbsp oregano, chopped
- 2 lb summer squash, diced
- 1 tbsp lime juice
- 1 c crumbled feta cheese
- 1 c quinoa
- 1 tsp salt
- ½ c onion, chopped
- 1 bell pepper, chopped
- 1 pint cherry tomatoes
- 12 oz tomatillos, husked and chopped

Directions:

1. Mix together the salt, lime juice, onion, pepper, tomatoes, and tomatillos.

2. Spray you cooker with nonstick spray. Place ingredients in the following layers: quinoa, cheese, and squash, and top with more cheese. Place the tomatillo mixture over everything. Don't stir everything together.

3. Set to slow cooker for 4 hours on low. Top with more cheese and oregano.

Spaghetti

Total Preparation & Cook Time: 3 hours 25 minutes

Servings – 8

Nutritional info: Calories: 302, Fats: 13 g, Carbs: 33g, Protein: 8g, Sugar: 0g, Sodium: 633mg

Ingredients:

- 3 oz parmesan
- 4 oz fontina cheese
- 1 tbsp oil
- package shredded mozzarella
- package shred cheddar
- 24 oz jar fire roasted tomato sauce
- 2 tsp garlic, minced
- 8 oz container onion/pepper mix
- 1 lb Italian sausage
- 8 oz spaghetti

Directions:

1. Brown the garlic, pepper mix, and sausage in a skillet.
2. Mix everything in the cooker. Set to slow cook for 3 hours on low.
3. Top with extra cheese.

Chapter 6 – Pasta & Grains

Spicy Lasagna

Total Preparation & Cook Time: 9 hours 10 minutes

Servings – 8

Nutritional info: Calories: 391, Fats: 15 g, Carbs: 34 g, Protein: 26g, Sugar: 11g, Sodium: 768mg

Ingredients:

- ½ c mozzarella
- ½ c water
- 12 no boil lasagna noodles
- 1 tsp oregano
- 3 ½ c chunky pasta sauce
- 10 oz chopped spinach
- 1 ¾ c Italian five cheese blend
- 15 oz ricotta cheese
- ¼ tsp crushed red pepper
- 12 oz ground turkey

Directions:

1. Brown the turkey in a skillet, breaking it up as it cooks. Take off the heat and mix in the red pepper and oregano.

2. Mix together the spinach, Italian cheese, and ricotta.

3. Place a cup of the sauce in the cooker. Put the noodles over the sauce. Add turkey mixture. More sauce and part of the water. Continue this pattern until you run out of ingredients.

4. Set to slow cook for 4 hours on low. Top with cheese.

Wild Mushroom Alfredo

Total Preparation & Cook Time: 2 hours 6 minutes

Servings – 8

Nutritional info: Calories: 234, Fats: 10 g, Carbs: 35 g, Protein: 6g, Sugar: 3g, Sodium: 652mg

Ingredients:

- 4 c baby spinach
- pepper
- 1 c walnut halves
- 4 c grape tomatoes
- 1 c parmesan
- 9 oz wild mushroom Agnolotti pasta
- 15 oz Alfredo sauce

Directions:

1. Place some Alfredo sauce in the cooker. Layer with one package of pasta, ½ cup parmesan, 2 cup tomatoes, and walnuts. Season with pepper and continue layering until ingredients are gone. Cover with Alfredo sauce.
2. Set to slow cook for 2 hours on high.

Wild Rice with Corn

Total Preparation & Cook Time: 4 hours 25 minutes

Servings – 12

Nutritional info: Calories: 119, Fats: 6 g, Carbs: 15 g, Protein: 3g, Sugar: 3g, Sodium: 101mg

Ingredients:

- 1/3 c basil
- ¾ c pecans
- 2 ¼ c boiling water
- ½ tsp salt
- ¾ c corn
- 1 ½ c onion, chopped
- ¾ c wild rice
- 2 ½ c sweet peppers, chopped
- nonstick spray
- 2 garlic cloves, minced
- 2 tsp oil

Directions:

1. Cook the garlic and the onions in a skillet until tender.
2. Spray the cooker with nonstick spray. Place in the salt, corn, rice, peppers, and onion mixture. Mix together with the boiling water.
3. Set to slow cook for 4 hours on low.

CHAPTER 7 – SEAFOOD

Amazing Mussels

Total Preparation & Cook Time: 1 hours 10 minutes

Servings – 4

Nutritional info: Calories: 413, Fats: 13.8 g, Carbs: 27.2 g, Protein: 24g, Sugar: 0g, Sodium: 1109mg

Ingredients:

- 5 lb mussels
- ½ c light cream
- 1 tbsp cornstarch
- 2 c white wine
- 20 basil leaves, torn
- 4 tomatoes, chopped
- 2 tbsp butter
- 1 chili pepper, minced
- jalapeno, minced
- 4 c beef broth
- 4 shallots, chopped
- 3 tbsp garlic, minced

Directions:

1. Cook shallots and garlic until a little browned. Mix in the pepper, jalapeno, and broth and let the flavors blend.

2. Pour into the cooker with wine, basil, and tomatoes. Set to slow cooker for 20 minutes on high.

3. Mix the cream and cornstarch together and stir into the mixture. Place the mussels into the liquid, and cook

another 40 minutes. Check periodical to see when they have opened.

Fisherman's Wharf Seafood

Total Preparation & Cook Time: 9 hours 55 minutes

Servings – 6

Nutritional info: Calories: 180, Fats: 6 g, Carbs: 10 g, Protein: 22g, Sugar: 5g, Sodium: 430mg

Ingredients:

- 2 tbsp parsley, chopped
- ¼ tsp hot sauce
- ½ tsp salt
- 2 tbsp oil
- 1 tsp basil
- 1 tsp sugar
- ½ lb shrimp, cleaned
- 1 lb tilapia, diced
- 1 bottle clam juice
- bay leaf
- ½ tsp fennel seed
- 1 c dry white wine
- 2 garlic cloves, chopped
- ½ c green bell pepper, chopped
- 3 c Italian plum tomatoes, quartered
- 1 c baby carrots, sliced
- 1 c leek, sliced

Directions:

1. In your cooker mix together the garlic, leek, and oil. Place in the clam juice, wine, bay leaf, fennel, pepper, tomatoes, and carrots. Mix well.

2. Set to slow cook for 8-9 hours on low.

3. Mix in the hot sauce, salt, basil, sugar, shrimp, and tilapia. Change temp to high and cook 20 minutes. Take out the bay leaf.

Chapter 6 – Pasta & Grains

Lemon and Herb Cod

Total Preparation & Cook Time: 2 hours 30 minutes

Servings – 4

Nutritional info: Calories: 110, Fats: 5 g, Carbs: 2 g, Protein: 25 g, Sugar: 0g, Sodium: 130mg

Ingredients:

- lemons
- ¼ c water
- ½ lemon, juiced
- 2 tbsp herbs de Provence
- 4 cod fillets

Directions:

1. Place the water in your cooker.
2. Lay the fish in the pot.
3. Season with the lemon juice and herbs de Provence, and pepper and salt.
4. Set to slow cook for 2 hours on low.

Paella

Total Preparation & Cook Time: 3 hours 13 minutes

Servings – 6

Nutritional info: Calories: 341, Fats: 5 g, Carbs: 47 g, Protein: 28g, Sugar: 0g, Sodium: 533mg

Ingredients:

- lemon wedge
- 1 ½ tsp garlic salt
- 1 ½ c vegetable broth
- 1 lb seafood medley
- 1 ½ c diced tomatoes
- 1 tsp turmeric
- ½ tsp paprika
- 1 bell pepper, chopped
- 1 c peas
- 1 onion, chopped
- 1 ½ c long grain brown rice
- 3 oz chicken sausage

Directions:

1. Brown the sausage in a skillet for a few minutes.
2. Place the spices, salt, broth, tomatoes, pepper, onion, rice, and chicken and mix in the cooker.
3. Set to slow cook. Let cook three hours on high.
4. Stir everything again. Add in the seafood mixture. Cook for 30 minutes on high.
5. Serve with lemon wedge.

Chapter 6 – Pasta & Grains

Salmon

Total Preparation & Cook Time: 2 hours 30 minutes

Servings – 4

Nutritional info: Calories: 60, Fats: 1 g, Carbs: 2 g, Protein: 20 g, Sugar: 0g, Sodium: 250mg

Ingredients:

- 1 ½ c liquid
- aromatic vegetables
- lemon
- spices
- pepper
- salt
- 2 lb salmon, skin on

Directions:

1. Cut salmon into serving pieces.
2. Season with pepper and salt and rub in.
3. Place parchment paper in your cooker to help you remove the salmon
4. Put the aromatics in the bottom of the pot.
5. Put a layer of salmon on top with the skin down.

6. If you have a lot of salmon and it won't all fit in one layer, put another piece of parchment paper down, more aromatics, and another layer of salmon.

7. Pour in your liquid.

8. Set to slow cook for 2 hours on low.

Seafood Stew

Total Preparation & Cook Time: 8 hours 15 minutes

Servings – 6

Nutritional info: Calories: 181, Fats: 1.5 g, Carbs: 16.5 g, Protein: 26g, Sugar: 4.5g, Sodium: 552mg

Ingredients:

- ½ c scallions, chopped
- ¼ c instant mashed potatoes
- bay leaf
- 8 oz large shrimp, cleaned
- 1 c onion, chopped
- 1 lb cod, diced
- 2 tsp thyme
- 1 tbsp garlic, chopped
- 2 c kale, chopped
- oz clams in juice
- 14.5 oz stewed tomatoes
- 3 ½ c vegetable broth

Directions:

1. Mix everything in the cooker except for the scallion and instant potatoes.
2. Set to slow cook for 7-8 hours on low.
3. Mix in the scallions and potato flakes, and discard the bay leaf.

Shrimp and Grits

Total Preparation & Cook Time: 7 hours 30 minutes

Servings – 4

Nutritional info: Calories: 476, Fats: 12.4 g, Carbs: 53.4 g, Protein: 36.3g, Sugar: 0g, Sodium: 1,060mg

Ingredients:

- Sirach
- salt
- 3 tbsp butter
- ½ c mozzarella
- ½ c cheddar
- 1 tbsp chili seasoning
- ¾ c pepper onion blend
- 2 garlic cloves, minced
- 10 oz raw shrimp, cleaned
- 2 andouille sausage, chopped
- c water
- 1 vegetable bouillon cube
- 1.5 c grits

Directions:

1. Put the sausage, water, bouillon, and grits in the cooker. Set to slow cook 4-5 hours on low.
2. Place the remaining ingredients in the pot, and cook 2 more hours.
3. Serve with Sirach.

Chapter 6 – Pasta & Grains

Shrimp Boil

Total Preparation & Cook Time: 8 hours 30 minutes

Servings – 6

Nutritional info: Calories: 450, Fats: 10 g, Carbs: 10 g, Protein: 33 g, Sugar: 0g, Sodium: 423mg

Ingredients:

- 4 c water
- 1 ½ lb shrimp, unpeeled
- 1 ½ tbsp old bay
- 1 ½ oz crab boil seasoning bag
- 8 mini corn cobs
- 2 ½ lb small potatoes
- 1 lb smoked sausage

Directions:

1. Slice sausage into chunks and put in a bag
2. Keep the boil bag together.
3. Place the crab boil, old bay, corn cobs, and potatoes into the sausage bag and coat.
4. Put everything in the bag in your cooker and pour in the water. Set to slow cook for 6-8 hours on low.
5. Mix in the shrimp and cook 30 minutes.

Shrimp Creole

Total Preparation & Cook Time: 1 hours 15 minutes

Servings – 4

Nutritional info: Calories: 290, Fats: 8 g, Carbs: 32 g, Protein: 21g, Sugar: 5g, Sodium: 498mg

Ingredients:

- 2 c cooked rice
- 2 tbsp parsley
- ¼ tsp salt
- 1 oz diced tomatoes
- 2 tbsp butter
- 2 garlic cloves, minced
- 1/8 tsp cayenne
- ½ c sweet pepper
- ½ c celery, chopped
- onion, chopped
- 1 lb shrimp, cleaned
- ½ tsp paprika

Directions:

1. Mix everything except for the shrimp in the pot. Set to slow cook. Let cook 40 minutes on low.
2. Place the shrimp and cook additional 20 minutes.

Chapter 6 – Pasta & Grains

Shrimp Scampi

Total Preparation & Cook Time: 1 hours 31 minutes

Servings – 4

Nutritional info: Calories: 256, Fats: 14.7 g, Carbs: 2.1 g, Protein: 23.3g, Sugar: 0g, Sodium: 466mg

Ingredients:

- 1 lb raw shrimp, cleaned
- 2 tbsp oil
- 2 tbsp parsley
- pepper
- 2 tbsp butter
- salt
- 1 tbsp lemon juice
- ½ c white cooking wine
- 1 tbsp garlic, minced
- ¼ c chicken broth

Directions:

1. Mix together the pepper, salt, lemon juice, parsley, garlic, butter, oil, wine, and broth in your cooker.
2. Mix in the shrimp.
3. Set to slow cook for 2 ½ hours on low.

Spicy Citrus Fish

Total Preparation & Cook Time: 3 hours 15 minutes

Servings – 6

Nutritional info: Calories: 374, Fats: 3.8 g, Carbs: 30.3 g, Protein: 52.9g, Sugar: 0g, Sodium: 505.5mg

Ingredients:

- your choice of fish
- pineapple salsa
- orange juice
- coconut milk
- fresh vegetables of your choosing

Directions:

1. Put the vegetables in the bottom of your cooker. Pour over the juices and part of the salsa.
2. Set to slow cook for 2 ½ hours on low.
3. Put the rest of the salsa in the pot with the fish. Set to high and cook 40 minutes.

Chapter 6 – Pasta & Grains

Steamed Mussels

Total Preparation & Cook Time: 1 hours 10 minutes

Servings – 4

Nutritional info: Calories: 250, Fats: 8 g, Carbs: 14.1 g, Protein: 27.5g, Sugar: 0g, Sodium: 998mg

Ingredients:

- ¼ c parsley, chopped
- ½ c dry white wine
- 2 lb mussels
- ¼ tsp pepper
- ¼ tsp salt
- Serrano chili, chopped
- ¼ c shallots, minced
- 1 tbsp butter

Directions:

Put everything the cooker. Set to slow cook and set for an hour on low. Check periodical and stop cooking once the mussels have opened.

CHAPTER 8 – DESSERTS

Caramel Pear Pudding Cake

Total Preparation & Cook Time: 4 hours 20 minutes

Servings – 16

Nutritional info: Calories: 201, Fats: 5 g, Carbs: 37 g, Protein: 2 g, Sugar: 24g, Sodium: 157 mg

Ingredients:

- 2 tbsp butter
- ¾ c brown sugar
- 2 tsp baking powder
- ½ c dried pears
- 2 c AP flour
- ¼ c oil
- 2 tbsp flax seed meal
- 1 tsp cinnamon
- 1 c milk
- 1 c pear nectar
- ½ tsp salt
- 2/3 c sugar
- nonstick spray
- 1 c water

Directions:

1. Spray the cooker with nonstick spray.
2. Mix together the salt, cinnamon, baking powder, flax seed, sugar, and flour together. Stir in the oil and milk. Fold in pears and pour into the cooker.
3. Mix the butter, brown sugar, nectar, and water in a pot until it boil. Pour on top of the batter.
4. Set to slow cook for 3 ½ hours on low.

Chapter 6 – Pasta & Grains

Crustless Lemony Cheesecake

Total Preparation & Cook Time: 8 hours 30 minutes

Servings – 8

Nutritional info: Calories: 253, Fats: 19 g, Carbs: 15 g, Protein: 6 g, Sugar: 0g, Sodium: 159mg

Ingredients:

- 1 c warm water
- 2 tsp lemon peel
- 3 eggs, beaten
- ½ c sour cream
- ½ tsp vanilla
- 1 tbsp AP flour
- 2 tbsp lemon juice
- ½ c sugar
- 12 oz cream cheese, softened
- nonstick spray

Directions:

1. Spray a soufflé dish with nonstick spray. Fix a foil sling under the dish.
2. Mix together the vanilla, flour, lemon juice, sugar, and cream cheese. Mix in the sour cream and then the eggs. Fold in the lemon peel.
3. Place batter in the dish. Cover with foil. Place the water in the cooker. Ease the dish into the cooker.
4. Set to slow cook for 2 ¼ hours on high.
5. Carefully remove the dish and let cool.

Ginger Orange Cheesecake

Total Preparation & Cook Time: 3 hours

Servings – 10

Nutritional info: Calories: 161, Fats: 8 g, Carbs: 17 g, Protein: 6g, Sugar: 14g, Sodium: 159mg

Ingredients:

- 2 blood oranges, sliced
- 1 c warm water
- 3 eggs, beaten
- ½ c sour cream
- ½ tsp vanilla
- 1 tbsp AP flour
- 2 tbsp orange juice
- 1 tsp orange peel
- ½ c sugar
- 12 oz cream cheese, softened
- cooking spray

Directions:

1. Spray a casserole dish that will fit in your cooker with nonstick spray. Make a foil sling to place on the bottom.

2. Beat vanilla, flour, orange juice, sugar, and cream cheese together. Mix in the sour cream and then eggs. Fold in the orange peel. Pour filling into the dish. Cover with foil.

3. Place the water into the cooker and ease the dish, with the sling, into the cook.

4. Set to slow cooker for 2 ½ hours on high. Take out the dish with the slings, and allow to cool.

Hazelnut Pudding Cake

Total Preparation & Cook Time: 3 hours 15 minutes

Servings – 10

Nutritional info: Calories: 550, Fats: 27 g, Carbs: 73 g, Protein: 8 g, Sugar: 52g, Sodium: 250mg

Ingredients:

- 2 chocolate hazelnut spread
- 2 tbsp hazelnut liqueur
- 1 ½ c boiling water
- ¾ c cocoa powder
- ¾ c sugar
- ½ c chocolate hazelnut spread
- ½ c hazelnuts, chopped
- ¼ c water
- 2 eggs
- ½ c butter, melted
- 18.4 oz fudge brownie mix
- nonstick spray

Directions:

1. Spray your cooker with nonstick spray.
2. Mix together fudge mix, butter, eggs, and water. Mix in ½ cup hazelnuts. Pour into the booker. Drop in the hazelnut spread and swirl with a knife.
3. Mix together the cocoa powder and sugar. Add in the liqueur and boiling water. Place on top of the batter. Set to slow cook for 2 ½ hours on low.

Chapter 8 – Desserts

Orange Caramel Pudding Cake

Total Preparation & Cook Time: 5 hours 30 minutes

Servings – 6

Nutritional info: Calories: 390, Fats: 15 g, Carbs: 61 g, Protein: 5 g, Sugar: 42g, Sodium: 255mg

Ingredients:

- chopped pecans
- caramel ice cream topping
- 1 tbsp butter
- ¾ c orange juice
- 2/3 c brown sugar, packed
- 1 tsp baking powder
- ½ tsp orange peel
- ¾ c water
- ¼ c raisins
- 1 c AP flour
- ½ c pecans, chopped
- 2 tbsp butter, melted
- ½ c milk
- ¼ tsp salt
- ½ tsp cinnamon
- 1/3 c sugar
- nonstick spray

Directions:

1. Spray your cooker with nonstick spray.
2. Mix together the salt, cinnamon, baking powder, sugar, and flours. Mix in the butter and milk. Fold in raisins and ½ cup pecans. Pour batter into cooker.

3. Mix together 1 tbsp butter, brown sugar, orange juice, orange peel, and water in a pot. Boil for about 2 minutes them pout into the cooker.

4. Set to slow cook for 4 ½ hours on low.

Chapter 8 – Desserts

Peach Graham Cracker Upside Down Cake

Total Preparation & Cook Time: 2 hours 40 minutes

Servings – 8

Nutritional info: Calories: 503, Fats: 19 g, Carbs: 78g, Protein: 6 g, Sugar: 48g, Sodium: 465mg

Ingredients:

- ¼ tsp grated nutmeg
- 1 c milk
- ¼ tsp salt
- 1 egg
- 2 c AP flour
- ½ c butter
- 1 c brown sugar
- ½ c brown sugar
- ½ c graham cracker, crushed
- 2 tsp ginger, grated
- 1 tsp baking soda
- ¼ c butter, softened
- 3 peaches, sliced
- nonstick spray

Directions:

1. Cook your cooker with nonstick spray. Place peaches in bottom. Mix sugar, butter, and ginger in a pot and melt the sugar and butter. Place over top of the peaches.

2. Mix the graham crackers and milk. Beat ½ cup butter and 1 cup brown sugar. Mix in the egg. Combine the flour, baking soda, salt and nutmeg. Mix together the wet, flour, and graham cracker mixture.

3. Pour over the peaches. Set to slow cook for 2 ½ hours on high.

Peppermint Pretzel Candies

Total Preparation & Cook Time: 2 hours

Servings – 48

Nutritional info: Calories: 151, Fats: 7 g, Carbs: 22 g, Protein: 1 g, Sugar: 13g, Sodium: 176mg

Ingredients:

- 3 oz dark chocolate, chopped
- ¾ c crushed peppermint
- 16 oz pretzel, chopped
- ½ tsp peppermint extract
- 3 tbsp butter
- 6 oz white caking chocolate, chopped
- 20 oz vanilla flavor candy coating, chopped

Directions:

1. Put a disposable liner in your cooker. Place in the butter, white chocolate, and candy coating. Mix well.
2. Set to slow cook for 1 ½ hours on low. Stir often. Mix in the extract, peppermint candies, and pretzels.
3. Place parchment paper on baking sheets. Place drops of the mixture on the baking sheets. Let stand until set.
4. Milk the dark chocolate and drizzle over the candies.

Chapter 8 – Desserts

Pumpkin Pomegranate Cheesecake

Total Preparation & Cook Time: 6 hours 40 minutes

Servings – 10

Nutritional info: Calories: 163, Fats: 8 g, Carbs: 18 g, Protein: 5 g, Sugar: 16g, Sodium: 151mg

Ingredients:

- ½ c pomegranate seeds
- 1 ½ tsp cornstarch
- 1 c warm water
- ½ tsp vanilla
- ½ c pomegranate juice
- 1 tbsp brown sugar
- 1 tsp orange peel
- 3 eggs, beaten
- 2/3 c canned pumpkin
- ½ tsp pumpkin pie spice
- 1 tbsp AP flour
- ½ c sugar
- 12 oz cream cheese, softened

Directions:

1. Mix everything together and pour into a prepared soufflé dish.
2. Cook on high for 2 hours.

Raspberry Fudge Brownies

Total Preparation & Cook Time: 3 hours 40 minutes

Servings – 12

Nutritional info: Calories: 204, Fats: 11 g, Carbs: 26 g, Protein: 2 g, Sugar: 0g, Sodium: 109mg

Ingredients:

- ¼ tsp baking powder
- ¾ c AP flour
- 1/3 c raspberry jam
- ½ c butter
- ¾ c sugar
- 2 eggs
- 1 tsp vanilla
- 2 oz unsweetened chocolate

Directions:

1. Grease 2 pint mason jars.
2. Melt the chocolate and butter. Mix in the vanilla, jam, sugar, and eggs. Mix in the baking powder and flour. Pour into the jars. Cover with foil. Put the jars in the cooker with a cup of water.
3. Set to slow cook for 3 ½ hours on high.

Chapter 8 – Desserts

Triple Chocolate Pudding Cake

Total Preparation & Cook Time: 3 hours

Servings – 8

Nutritional info: Calories: 372, Fats: 15 g, Carbs: 52 g, Protein: 5g, Sugar: 26g, Sodium: 125mg

Ingredients:

- 1 ½ c boiling water
- 2 tbsp cocoa powder
- ¾ c sugar
- ½ c peanuts, chopped
- 2 tbsp cocoa powder
- ½ c semisweet chocolate pieces
- 1 c AP flour
- ½ c peanut butter pieces
- 2 tsp vanilla
- 1 ½ tsp baking powder
- 2 tbsp oil
- ½ c chocolate milk
- 1/3 c sugar
- nonstick spray

Directions:

1. Spray your cooker with nonstick spray.
2. Mix together baking powder, 2 tbsp cocoa powder, 1/3 c sugar, and flour. Mix in the vanilla, oil, and milk. Fold in the peanuts, chocolate pieces, and peanut butter pieces. Pour into the cooker.
3. Mix together 2 tbsp cocoa powder and ¾ cup sugar. Mix in the boiling water and pour over the batter the is in the cooker.
4. Set to slow cook for 2 ½ hours on high.

Made in the USA
San Bernardino, CA
12 February 2017